AF316680

The Weekly Reset

Written by Brendt and Kim Wills

Copyright © 2022

Images by: iStock and Kim Wills

ISBN 9798218109684

Library of Congress Control Number 2022923419

Printed in the United States of America by
Ingram Spark/Lightning Source

Published by Spirit Wings Designs 2022
daslpacker55@yahoo.com

The
Weekly
Reset

Shabbat שַׁבָּת

Dedication

This book is dedicated to "you", the ones willing to take the information in this book and apply it. You will be changing generations to come. Take the secret decoder ring and unlock the potential of your family and relationships closest to you.

Thank You

Thank you Cindy Snell for editing this book. Your friendship, prayers and kindness are one of our most highly valued assets. Your willingness to wade through the things that I send you to edit is priceless. We love you, Brendt and Kim. Oh, and thanks for making me sound smart.

Thank you Jan Asleson of Spirit Wings Designs. Kim and I are so grateful for your friendship, care and willingness to design and publish this book. We have repeatedly encountered your encouragement in many ways. The encouragement that you provide for key leaders in the body of messiah is so powerful and needed! We love you, Brendt and Kim.

Important Instructions:

I am well aware that many homes are missing certain agents that the father intended to be present. A missing father figure does not negate the need for a father's blessing weekly. Who is the father representing? He is representing God the Father, who is the one who is formulating the blessing anyway. If there is a father figure in the house he should be listening to Holy Spirit to receive the words to pronounce in blessing over each individual. The enemy has stolen these safeguards out of our culture, let's put an end to that.

What part of the Godhead does the woman of the house represent? I believe the Holy Spirit is who she is to reveal to her house and to her family. Just because there is not a mother figure in the the home does not change the fact that the Holy Spirit is the light of that home. If a father was to light the Shabbat candles could not the family receive the presence of the Holy Spirit into their home? Of course! Let's not over complicate the process, remember Balaam's donkey.

Kim and I have modeled the Shabbat blessings in many different churches and homes. We always instruct the ladies who are not married to receive the husband's blessing as if God the Father was personally speaking the words over them. In the same way we instruct the men to receive the blessing over the husband either in preparation for marriage or leadership.

We first started engaging in the Shabbat blessing when our daughters were in college. It was amazing to me how many of their friends would come every Friday night to receive a blessing. Likewise we have been teaching on this subject and have pulled an older person up to pray a father's blessing over them. A good portion of the time they were old enough to be our father or mother but the blessing was just as impactful and life-changing.

I will never forget what I learned in CPR years ago. The instructor told us not to worry about messing something up because doing something is better than doing nothing at all. Our culture is on life support. We have nearly flatlined. So doing something is far better than doing nothing. If you're worried you may mess something up, don't worry, you probably will. But the blessing that person receives through your obedience will be life-changing!

Introduction

I would like to share with you
what we have been taught from
the 'beginning' was void of the
'decoder ring' of culture, history,
and the fullness of His Torah.

The same Torah which will
also be taught by Yeshua in
the Millennial reign!
(Isaiah 2:3)

The Shabbat meal is completely Rabbinical (please allow me to explain why I am addressing this). There are two different levels of understanding: (1) Biblical (of or in the Bible), and (2) Rabbinical (of or relating to rabbis, their learning and writings, etc.) We, as believers, have completely discarded anything that is Rabbinical. I believe that is due to being overly concerned that we would somehow violate God's word in following these guidelines. It may be similar to a person desiring to master the game of basketball. Michael Jordan agrees to assist them in pursuit. However, we keep telling him that the rule book says nothing about planting your foot in a certain manner before a layup or the positioning of your tongue in your mouth. We probably would all agree that this would seem ridiculous! Similarly, we have done the same thing to the only people who understand the culture of the Bible.

The purpose of this book is to reconnect the body of Yeshua to a structure that was intended to be a RESET for life. Our culture has stripped away the strength intended to be evident in every family submitted to the Lord. The Shabbat was the first measure established published by God to ensure a life filled with freedom and power. (Genesis 2:1-3, Leviticus 23:1-3).

As a father, I remember initially being introduced to the 'concept' of Shabbat. It was described as something they practiced back in 'Bible times'. Unfortunately, I did not understand that it was not something to only be utilized centuries ago, but is something to continue using here and now. This was no fault of the presenter, but was due to an ingrained pattern of my own thinking, being that everything in the Old Testament had been done away with. Oh, you fell for that too, oops.

I am a grandfather of six, and looking back on my life, I realize that my family is a far cry from the generational garbage that I grew up in. However, the understanding of the Shabbat could have generated so much more life into my own children. My grandchildren have immensely less garbage to battle. I am blessed because my grandchildren walk in deeper generational blessing then their own parents did.

Isaiah 57:14 has been a life scripture for me. And it will be said, "Build up, build up, prepare the way, Remove every obstacle out of the way of My people."

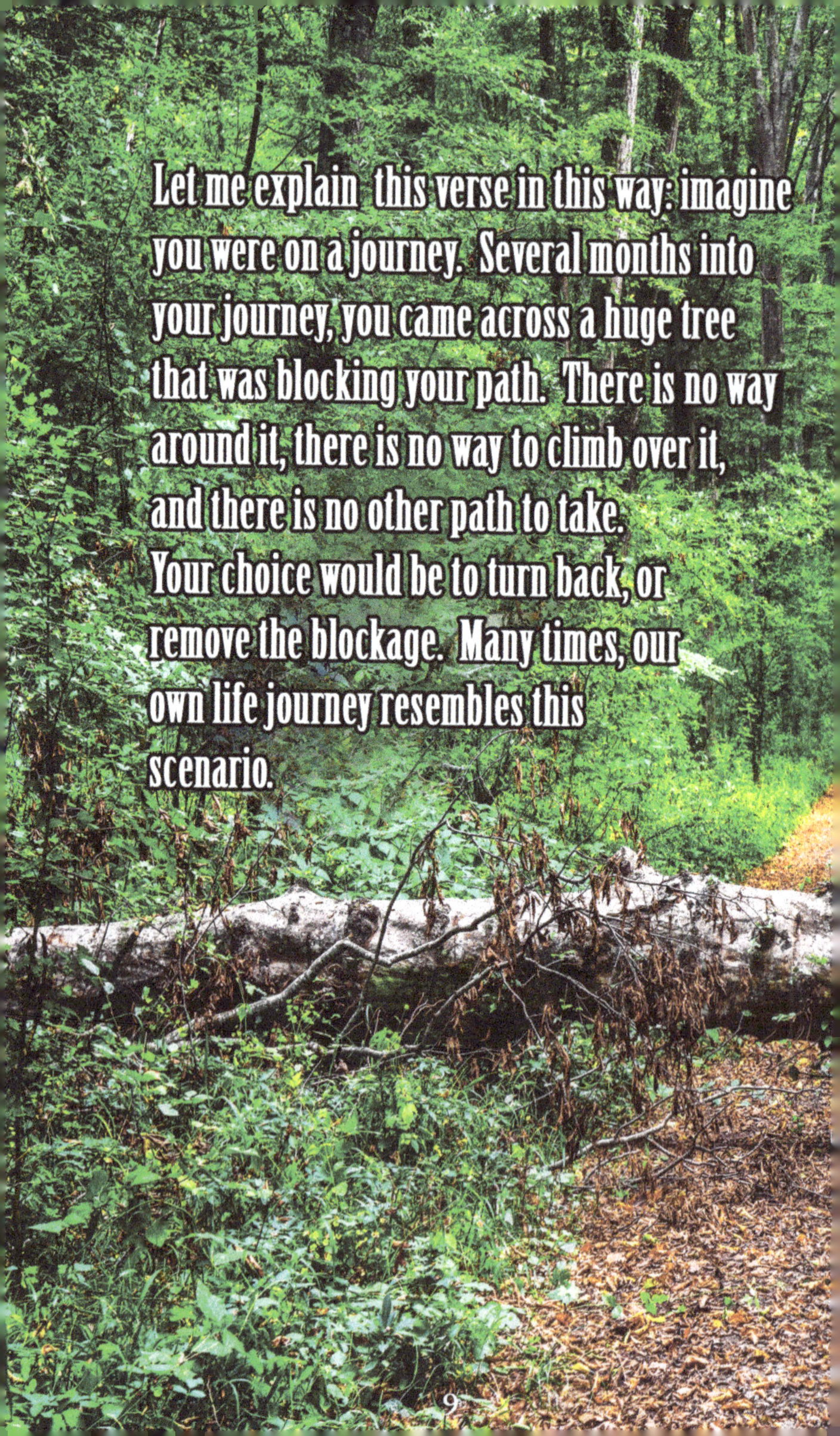

Let me explain this verse in this way: imagine
you were on a journey. Several months into
your journey, you came across a huge tree
that was blocking your path. There is no way
around it, there is no way to climb over it,
and there is no other path to take.
Your choice would be to turn back, or
remove the blockage. Many times, our
own life journey resembles this
scenario.

There are three kinds of people I want you to reflect on. The first type of person might say, "If I knew there was going to be an obstacle in my journey, I never would have begun the journey". This person sits down on the trail and gives up. Travelers, visionaries, and persons less educated than himself pass by on the path. He is now unable to move because the obstacle is more massive in his mind than it is in reality. His inability to move forward has blinded him from the fact that others have found a way through the trail.

The second type of person is one who has been enjoying the journey. He comes to the block-age with an inability to persevere through the process of its removal. This person gives up on the journey, turns around, and heads towards home. The victories gained by completing the journey are stolen not only from him, but also from all of his future generations as well. What could have been gained at the end of the journey and may have produced generational blessings will never be received.

The third type of person has been enjoying the journey and is agitated by the obstacle.

This person hits the obstacle head-on with a sense of purpose that is focused with future, goals and completing the journey. He understands that his journey is about far more than his own desires or needs. The destiny of his journey is only the middle of his children's journey and may be only the beginning of his grandchildren's journey. What he chooses to go through has a direct correlation with their successes.

Obviously, each person has the ability to choose to avert obstacles. We do not carry the weight of other's choices , but have to 'own up' to our personal decisions/actions. We desire to set future generations on a winning course! If you are like me, not having achieved the 'walking on the water thing', you probably made a few mistakes along the way. Isaiah 57:14 relays to us that we cannot turn around and go back. We cannot sit on the trail and pout, but we must press throught the obstacles. Is it too late? Never! When you first see the obstacle, that is the specifically ordained time for you to deal with it. If you have been looking at the same obstacle for years, "now" is still the time to deal with it. Let me encourage you…it feels great on the other side! In Kansas, we have hedge trees which are covered in giant thorns that seem to have some type of oily substance on them, ensuring the most pain from each prick. Pioneers used them as fences because nothing or no one wanted to pass through them. Those hedge rows are akin to fear: you will have to pass through the idea of the pain you know you will encounter to receive the victory waiting on the other side of the barrier.

The purpose of the weekly Shabbat is to continue to build up, prepare the way, and remove the obstacles in a generational manner. As I mentioned earlier, our culture has stripped away the strength intended to be evident in every family submitted to the Lord. In my opinion, the weekly Shabbat is the best way to do this by removing the obstacles that break down our family units.

A recent series called "The Chosen" depicts the Shabbat being celebrated in every home. Even Yeshua/Jesus enjoys the weekly Shabbat! Sadly, we have missed a very simple verse that our Savior spoke. That verse is a small picture of how to keep God's culture in our culture. That verse is John 5:19: "Therefore Jesus answered and was saying to them, 'Truly, truly, I say to you, the Son can do nothing of Himself, unless it is something He sees the Father doing; for whatever the Father does, these things the Son also does in like manner.

Unfortunately, due to some very poor teaching, we have been convinced that the Son came to do away with the things the Father was doing. That could not be further from the truth. There is an old saying that says, "If it's not broke, don't fix it."

This book is a guide to reinstate the safeguards intended to be experienced throughout the coming generations. Please understand that I personally do not know everything about Shabbat. We, in the body of Messiah, have just recently started listening to our older brothers whom we call Jews, not realizing that we belong to the same family. As we allow their ancient understanding to reshape our culture, we will then truly understand **His** culture. We pray that you and your family are blessed as you keep the Shabbat (Exodus 20:8-10)

What Is Shabbat?

Shabbat, in Hebrew, means to rest. In our busy
world, we rarely rest as God has commanded us
 to do. If you think about it, the God of the universe,
who could do anything He wanted to, stopped on
the seventh day and rested. He then invited us to
 join Him each week to do the same.

One of the ways Yeshua honored the Shabbat was by waiting until the next day to rise from the dead. Mark 28:1 "In the end of the sabbath, as it began to dawn toward the first day of the week, came Mary Magdalene and the other Mary to see the sepulcher.

I am writing this book during the Covid-19 quarantine. I am sure that the future will hold many insights about this time of history. One thing that we have learned during this time is how to rest and re-connect with our families. The treadmill of life has been shut down, and all that is left at the end of the day is what is 'real'. When driving by a pond in Southeast Kansas at a high rate of speed, it might look quite lovely. When you slow down, you realize that it is not a pond…it is a sewage lagoon, and not lovely at all. The speed of your life changes your perception, and often our vision gets blurred. I'm sure that many people realize their lack of rest and reconnection has cost them greatly. I know that the Father is getting a lot of mileage out of this time.

When you breakdown the word Shabbat into the Hebrew letters, שַׁבָּת it could be translated "return to covenant." What covenents are we returning to? The covenants that are reflected in our numerous and varied types of relationships.

Why do we need to return to these covenants? As
Ephesians 4:13 alludes to, we have not reached
the full measure and stature of maturity. In other
words, we chip away at these relationships every
day. The result, if left unchecked, could be a vast
separation growing between persons unnoticed.
Loving couples divorce after 40 years of marriage,
teens rebel against their parents, and most
importantly, we find ourselves numb to the Rauch
ha Kodesh (the Holy Spirit).

Each blessing given during the Shabbat meal is
intended to cause you to examine that specific
relationship. By doing this weekly, you are safe-
guarding against permanent relational damage.
Before speaking each blessing, check with the one
you are blessing and ask if there are any breaches in
your relationship. If there is an offense, deal with
it quickly! You cannot bless someone that you are
at odds with. Imagine a child growing up in a
home that practices this weekly…there is virtually
no place for rebellion to maintain a foothold in the
family.

Read Isaiah 57:14. After the obstacle is removed,
the blessing will have a place to settle. You have to
remove the roadblocks before you can travel down

the road. We want to bless those we are in covenant
with, but our actions and attitudes place debris in
their path. Don't keep the blessing we intended for
them 'stuck in traffic'. With a clear road, that blessing
will get to the destination.

The most important relationship we examine weekly
is the one between our Father God and each of us
individually.

Isaiah 58:13 "If you turn away your foot from the
Sabbath, From doing your pleasure on My holy day,
And call the Sabbath a delight, The holy day of the
Lord honorable, And shall honor Him, not doing your
own ways, Nor finding your own pleaure, Nor speak-
ing your own words, 14 Then you shall delight yourself
in the Lord; And I will cause you to ride on the high
hills of the earth, And feed you with the heritage of
Jacob your father. The mouth of the Lord has spoken."
(NKJV)

Here, Father God is asking us to remove the obstacles
out of the way so that He may bless us. Not to only
bless you, but your family and future generations as
well…

One last thought for this intoduction: The Shabbat is
held on Friday evening with the anticipatin of resting

on Saturday. Shabbat begins at sundown of Friday and ends at sundown Saturday. Genesis chapter 1 says, "and it was evening, and it was morning the first day" and so on. The most significant portion of the reconnection that Shabbat affords us is the day of rest. Speaking the blessings and enjoying a meal together is the doorway for restoration that happens during this rest. The Shabbat meal is intended to remove the debris and obstacles in our minds so we may be restored to genuine fellowship with one another.

Getting Ready

Here are some suggestions on how to prepare for the evening. Please remember, Shabbat is a set apart time, so it should be special and you will need to decide what that specifically means for your family. You may choose to be very formal or casual; but either way, it is about reconnecting and enjoyment - do not let the preperation for the evening impede the mood.

1. Set the table. You may want to use fine China or just a tablecloth to make this meal set apart from other meals during the week.

2. You will need two white candles and a way to light them. Some unique candlestick holders might add to the ambiance of the evening. Our family has used oil lamps that someone brought us from Israel.

3. If Kim (my wife) is able, she likes to bake Challah bread. There is a simple recipe towards the back of the book. At other times we use a piece of bread, crackers, or rolls. We understand that we live in a busy world, and it is not always possible to bake bread, so please do not stress about it!

4. You might want to use special stemware to drink the wine or grape juice from. We have some tiny wine glasses that our grandchildren enjoy using specifically for Shabbat.

5. The evening meal can be varied. Sometimes we enjoy a large home-cooked meal and other times we may buy a pizza or our favorite fast food. And when we gather with a large group, everyone brings something to share. Whatever your choice, make sure that it is enjoyable and a blessing for all involved.

Setting the Atmosphere

Shabbat is somewhat of a formal dinner. With that in mind, you need to remember that the child that always spills **is** going to spill. Perhaps you can shelf etiquette training and enjoy the gift of your family along with the spills, messes, and all the other distractions.

During this meal, please be led by The Ruach ha Kodesh (Holy Spirit). The intent of the evening is to reconnect with the culture God intended. We are not starting some kind of new ritual. Shabbat is meant to be a healing, reconnecting, meal for you and your family.

Shabbat is like a slingshot - we are pulling back to be thrust forward! The weaker the pull back, the weaker the thrust. Concentrate on rest in your heart and attitude, have fun, and remember why you love your family. They are most definitely unique and chosen by the very hand of God for you!

Let me emphasize that many of us do not still have children living at home. That does not change the importance of or necessity to keep the weekly Shabbat. We continue to practice the weekly Shabbat even though all of our children are out of the house. We still need the weekly removal of 'debris' from our lives and the reconnection that God intended for both of us. We always pray each blessing over each other as the Spirit knows no distance or boundaries. No matter how old our children are, we want them blessed and able to continue to bless the next generations if they have their own children. When the extended family comes together on

Shabbat, we're in a unique position as grandparents. We're excited to pray the blessing over our children and even more so to hear them pray the blessings over their children.

If you want to modify or 'add to' any of the prayers, please do so. We pray that Shabbat becomes a blessing to you and your family, and not a burden to perform some kind of traditional program or ritual. Without the presence of Holy Spirit and the fellowship of our families, it becomes just 'another' family dinner.

Remember that each blessing during the Shabbat meal is intended to cause you to examine that specific relationship. Seek our Father's perspective for blind spots you may have. Your ability to clear the path enables the recipient to be built up, successful, and ready to truly celebrate this thing we call life!

Blessing to Welcome in the Shabbat And Lighting the Candles

Right before sunset, on Erev Shabbat (Friday evening) with excitement and anticipation, the woman of the house lights two Shabbat candles. She then extends her hands over the candles and draws them inwards three times in a circular motion and them she covers her eyes.

She continues speaking out the blessings, welcoming in the Shabbat.

Blessing

Blessed are You, Yehovah, our God, King of the
universe, Who sanctified us by Your commandments, and the blood of Messiah, Yeshua, and
commanded us to be a light for the nations
and gave us Yeshua our Messiah, the light of
the world.
Blessed are You, Yehovah, our God, King of the
universe, Who has sanctified us by Your
commandments and by the blood of Yeshua the
Messiah as we kindle the Shabbat lights.

Insight

It has been taught that the two candles represent
many things. Some say creation and redemption
are the two witnesses, but the one I prefer to use is
Jerusalem. In the word Jerusalem, the "em" ("im"
in Hebrew) indicates plural, Heavenly, and Earthly,
Jerusal-em. On Erev Shabbat, we are taking a
brief break from the earthly to connect with the
heavenly. The thought for the night is heaven
visiting earth, and we, here on earth, are visiting

a piece of heaven.

The woman of the house lights the candles because
it was a woman who brought forth Yeshua, the
Light of the World. The woman is the foundation
of the home.
She waves her hands three times to bring the light
of Shabbat in: first for herself, secondly for her
family, and lastly for the entire household.
(friends and family).

The lighting of the candles, just before sundown,
opens the Shabbat. Sometimes we close our eyes
during the lighting, and after the blessing, we open
them, making a clear transition between the
ordinary week and the Holy Shabbat.

Blessing Over the Shabbat

The father speaks the following verses
and blessing over the Shabbat.

Genesis 1:31 God saw all that He had made, and behold, it was very good. And there was evening and there was morning, the sixth day.

2:1 Thus the heavens and the earth were completed and all their hosts.

2:2 By the seventh day God completed His work which He had done, and He rested on the seventh day from all His work which He had done.

Blessing

Blessed are You, Yehovah, our God, Ruler of the universe, Who sanctified us by Your commandments and has taken pleasure in us, and in love and favor You have caused us to inherit the holy Shabbat in remembrance of the creation, a day on which You ceased from Your work; that day being also the first of Your holy feasts, and is a memorial of our departure from Egypt, even our personal "Egypt" of iniquity, sin and bondage. For You have chosen us and forgiven us our sins through the blood atonement of our Messiah Yeshua and in love and favor have invited us to inherit the Shabbat for rest and refreshing.

Peace be unto you, ministering angels, messengers

of the Most High, the King of kings, the Holy One,
blessed be He. May your coming be in peace,
messengers of the Most High, The King of kings, the
Holy One, blessed be He. May your departure be in
peace, messengers of peace, messengers of the Most
High, the King of kings, the Holy One, blessed be He.

The father then prays to settle the Shabbat over the
family.
**Everyone now greets each other by saying:
Shabbat Shalom! (Peaceful rest)**

Insight

Psalm 3:5 I lay down and slept; I awoke, for the Lord
sustains me. When we enter into His rest, He will
sustain us. Let go and relax. Then your Father will hold
the stuff of the week for you. Next, we need to show
some love. The love we need to show is to ourselves.
Lack of rest is the biggest trap the enemy sets for us.
When we can't love ourselves by resting and resetting
it disables us from loving others.

Mark 12:30 and you shall love the Lord your God with
all your heart, and with all your soul, and with all your
mind, and with all your strength. 31 The second is this
'You shall love your neighbor as yourself.' There is no
other commandment greater then these.

Blessings Over the Wife
and Husband

Blessing Over the Wife
Husband Prays a Blessing Over His Wife

Blessing From Proverbs 31

An excellant wife, who can find? (But I have found her in you.) For your worth is far above money or jewels. You look well to the ways of your household and do not eat the bread of idleness. Your children rise up and bless you. Your husband also, and he praises you saying: "Many daughters have been noble, but you exceed them all. A woman such as you, who fears Yehovah, she shall be praised."

After you pray this blessing over your wife, add another blessing from your own heart. Remind her that she is the love of your life and then speak over her words that build her up and edify her.

Insight

Shabbat is a built-in reset that strengthens marriages. The amount of debris that had to be removed off of our path was impressive. Each week as we walked through the process we were brought closer together. A large portion of the healing and freedom that I personally walk in arose from those times. Also, in the blessing where it says, "You look well to the ways of your household," I like to pause and 'stretch out', **you look well.** Give it a try…it works great for brownie points! Besides, your children should know that you still think she is amazing. Remind her that she still rocks your world!

Blessing Over the Husband
The Wife Prays a Blessing Over Her Husband

Blessing from Psalms 1:1-3

1. How blessed is the man who does not walk in the the path of sinners, nor sit in the seat of the scoffer.
2. But his delight is in the law of the Lord, And in His law he meditates day and night.
3. He will be like a tree firmly planted by streams of water, Which yields its fruit in its season And its leaf does not wither; And in whatever he does, he prospers.

After you pray this blessing over your husband, add another blessing from your own heart. Remind him that he is the love of your life and speak over him words that build him up.

Insight

When I, Kim, pray the blessing over Brendt, I focus on "Whatever he does, he prospers." For all areas of his life …spiritually, emotionally, physically, and financially. The added blessing is that I benefit as well. Because we are one, when he prospers, we prosper! I also thank the Father that I am blessed with a Godly husband, father, and papa for our family and that I would follow him as he follows Yehovah! We really enjoy celebrating Shabbat, so when I speak over my husband, we have fun! Not in an irreverent manner, but in a playful way because he is my best friend. As I speak out over Brendt, it reminds me of who God says he is.

Blessing Over the Children
The father prays a blessing over his children

Mothers, you may also play a part in this time of blessing as well. I would suggest that you, as a couple, decide what that looks like before the evening begins.

For Daughters: May Yehovah make you like Sarah and Rebekah, Rachel and Leah. (Queens and Princesses)

May Yehovah bless you and keep you. May Yehovah make His face to shine upon you, illuminate you with His presence, and grant you favor with all men and be gracious to you. May Yehovah lift His countenance upon you and give you shalom/peace. Numbers 6:24-26

For Sons: Genesis 41:51-51 & 48:20 May Yehovah make you like Ephraim and Manasseh. (Cause to forget and fruitful)

May Yehovah bless you and keep you. May Yehovah make His face to shine on you, illuminate you with His presence, and grant you favor with all men and be gracious to you. May Yehovah lift His countenance upon you and give you shalom/peace. Numbers 6:24-26

Pray blessings over your children and words that God has given you specifically for them during the week. Remind them they are a needed part of your family and a blessing to all in attendance. In many cases, they are an answer to your prayers to become parents.

Insight

During any given week teachers, friends and parents 'program' children. What children hear speaks to them about who they <u>are</u> and who they <u>are not</u> and these messages are building their identities. Through this weekly blessing as parents, we are resetting a child's identity, bringing it back into truth; that being what "The Father" has said about him/her. This is essential because it is a work in progress, yet "The Father" sees the finished product.

For the fathers: you are the agent set in place to represent Father God. As you set and reset identity, remember this fact: it is about what He says about your child.

Can you bless a child that has been misbehaving all week? Yes, if you keep in mind that you are blessing their God-given identity, not their actions. Identity pertains to who they are, and action pertains to what they are doing…this must be kept separate. When we bless our children, we should keep in mind two things: (1) To make His face to shine upon them and (2) lift up His countenance upon them. It is the picture of a father lifting up a child and looking up into his/her eyes and then blessing them…this is powerful!
Did you know that you look better when you look upward as opposed to when you look downward? Just ask anyone who has ever taken a selfie---your countenance changes when you look up. Your assignment when you are blessing your children is to reflect The Father.

You may need to kneel in front of them, repent for your shortcomings, and then bless them. Warning: your child might change right in front of your eyes!

Saying the Sh'ma Together

When we speak out the "Sh'ma", we are coming into agreement with Yehova's instructions that will bring about the life He intended for us. These instructions are found in Deuteronomy 6:4 and Mark 12:30

Together:

Sh'ma Yisrael Yehovah Elohainu, Yehovah Echad.
Hear Oh Israel, Yehovah, our God, Yehovah is One.
Deuteronomy 6:5-7.
You shall love Yehovah, your God with all your heart, with all your soul, with all your strength.
And these words which I command you today shall be in your heart.
You shall teach them diligently to your children, and shall talk of them when you sit in your house, when you walk by the way, when you lie down, and when you rise up.

Insight

In Deuteronomy 6:1-3, the Word gives us four promises, and verse 4-7 tells us how to achieve them. The four promises are: (1) generational, (2) prolonged life, (3) that it would be well with you, and (4) that you may multiply greatly.

The mere fact that you are reading this tells me that you are generationally minded. The idea of the life benefits of longevity, prosperity, and multiplying are byproducts of that mindset. The generations cry out for the previous one to lead them, so that they may inherit those benefits. Our individual walk cannot be taught to them. Our children must 'catch it', so to speak.

Sing Praises to the Lord

You might sing "Shabbat Shalom" (It's easy because those are the only words), or your favorite worship song.

Blessing Over the Wine, The Kiddush

Kiddush means sanctification, set aside, or special. The Kiddush is the cup of wine that is consumed during the shabbat meal. This cup is an image or visual reminder that we are entering into a special, set apart time, the Sabbath. Shabbat is different than all of the other six days. In our culture, especially in Christianity, we relate wine to drunkenness and/or debauchery. However, the Hebrew culture views consuming wine as a special and joyful experience... something that marks that time spent as different. When we drink the wine or grape juice, it likens to a bookmark that is holding our place on the page of 'rest'.

Blessing

Baruch Atah Yehovah, Elohainu melech ha-olam, bo-ray pre-hagafen. Blessed are You, Yehovah our God, King of the universe, Who creates the fruit of the vine.

This is a great time for the father to reinforce the understanding that we are members of the same family. We have been grafted into father Abraham, the olive tree. (Romans 11:17-25)

Say the following:

And on the night before He died, Yeshua took the cup and gave thanks, and gave it to them, saying, "Drink from it, all of you, for this is My blood of the new covenant, which is shed for many for the remission of sins. (Matthew 26:27-28)

Blessing Over the Challah Bread

The Challah is made of three strands of dough, which represents the Father, Son and the Holy Spirit. Two loaves speak of the double portion of manna that the Israelites gathered on the sixth day (Exodus 16:22), so they would not have to work on the Shabbat. The bread also depicts total reliance upon Yehovah for provision because we have chosen not to work.

The father uncovers the two loaves of Challah and, while holding them up, he recites the following:

Blessing

Baruch Atah Yehovah, Elohainu Melech ha-olam,
ha motzee lechem meen ha-aretz.
Blessed are You, Yehovah, our God, King of the
universe, Who brings forth bread from the earth.

The Father also speaks the following:

And ad they were eating, Yeshua took bread, blessed
and broke it, and gave to His disciples and said,
"Take, eat; this is My Body. (Matthew 26:26)
You can then break the loaves of the Challah and give
some to each person at the table. You may all eat some
of the bread at this time.

Blessing Over the Meal

Pray a blessing over the meal and
simply thank the Father for
His provision for your family.

Easy Challah Bread

Ingredients: per loaf

*   1 (.25 ounce) package active dry yeast
*   1 cup warm water (100 degrees F/40 degrees C)
*   2 tablespoons honey
*   1 teaspoon salt
*   3 beaten eggs
*   3 1/2 cups all-purpose flour, plus more for kneading
*   1 beaten egg yolk, or more if needed
*   1 tablespoon melted butter (optional)

Directions

1. In a large bowl, stir the yeast into the water and let the mixture stand until a creamy layer forms on the top, about 10 minutes. Stir in the honey and salt until dissolved, and add the beaten eggs. Mix the flour, a cupful at a time, until the dough is sticky. Sprinkle the mixture with flour, and knead until smooth and elastic, about 5 minutes.

2. Form the dough into a compact round shape, and place in an oiled bowl. Turn the dough over several times in the bowl to oil the surface of the dough,

cover the bowl with a damp cloth, and let rise in
a warm area until doubled in size, 45 minutes to
1 hour.

3. Punch down the dough and cut it into three equal-
   sized pieces. Working on a floured surface, roll the
   small dough pieces into ropes about the thickness of
   your thumb and about 12 inches long. Ropes should
   be fatter in the middle and thinner at the ends. pinch
   three ropes together at the top and braid them. Starting with the strand to the right, move it to the left,
   over the middle strand (that strand now becomes the
   new middle strand.) Take the strand farthest to the left,
   and move it over the new middle strand. Continue braid-
   ing, alternating sides each time, until the loaf is raised,
   and pinch the ends together and fold them underneath
   for a neat look.

4. Place the braided loaf on a baking sheet lined with
   parchment paper and brush the top with beaten
   egg yolk. (For a softer crust, brush with melted
   butter instead.)

5. Preheat oven to 350 degrees F (175 degrees C)

6. Bake the Challah in the preheated over until the
   top browns to a rich golden color, and the loaf
   sounds hollow when you tap it with a spoon, 30 to
   35 minutes. Cool on a wire rack before slicing.

Authors
Brendt & Kim Wills

Brendt and Kim Wills have been involved in many aspects of ministry since 1988. They have served as pastors, youth pastors, in children's ministry, Street ministry and prayer counseling. The Wills' have pastored Eagle Rock Ministries in Coffeyville, Kansas since 2005. Traveling coast to coast they have ministered in churches, home fellowships, small groups, parks, streets and reservations. If you were to ask the Wills' what their life scripture would be they would say, Isaiah 57:14 And it will be said "Build up, build up, prepare the way, Remove every obstacle from the way of My people."

* 9 7 9 8 2 1 8 1 0 9 6 8 4 *